NARROW GATE,
NARROW WAY

NARROW GATE,
NARROW WAY

Paul Washer

Reformation Heritage Books
Grand Rapids, Michigan

Narrow Gate, Narrow Way
© 2018 by Paul Washer

Reformation Heritage Books
3070 29th St. SE
Grand Rapids, MI 49512
616-977-0889
orders@heritagebooks.org
www.heritagebooks.org

Printed in the United States of America
21 22 23 24 25 26/10 9 8 7 6 5 4 3

Scripture taken from the New King James Version®. Copyright © 1982 by Thomas Nelson. Used by permission. All rights reserved.

Library of Congress Cataloging-in-Publication Data

Names: Washer, Paul, 1961- author.
Title: Narrow gate, narrow way / Paul Washer.
Description: Grand Rapids, Michigan : Reformation Heritage Books, 2018.
Identifiers: LCCN 2018027449 (print) | LCCN 2018029311 (ebook) | ISBN 9781601786302 (epub) | ISBN 9781601786296 (pbk. : alk. paper)
Subjects: LCSH: Bible. Matthew, VII, 13-27—Sermons.
Classification: LCC BS2575.54 (ebook) | LCC BS2575.54 .W37 2018 (print) | DDC 226.2/06—dc23
LC record available at https://lccn.loc.gov/2018027449

For additional Reformed literature, request a free book list from Reformation Heritage Books at the above regular or e-mail address.

Contents

The Author's Prayer

Father, I am so small and so pitiful in so many ways. I tremble lest false fire should be brought before Your altar. Yet what if fire came down from heaven, amid all the noise, clamor, and activities of the world? If fire would come down from heaven, then these dead bones would live. You know, O Lord.

I pray and I beg before the throne of God that in Your sovereignty You would be gracious to us, that You would open hearts and minds. Lord, we cannot wait for men and women to open theirs. They never will. Open up their hearts and minds and cause them to see biblical truth. Breathe on them. Grant them repentance. Grant them faith. Bring them into Your kingdom, Lord, for Your own glory, for the sake of Your own great name; do this thing, Lord. Let it come to pass, Lord, so that no man will take credit for it, so that no man will lay his hand to the ark of God and be struck down dead. Oh, God, move among us, please, because we have no other hope. These young people have no other hope except that You move. Amen.

Matthew 7:13–27

Enter by the narrow gate; for wide is the gate and broad is the way that leads to destruction, and there are many who go in by it. Because narrow is the gate and difficult is the way which leads to life, and there are few who find it.

Beware of false prophets, who come to you in sheep's clothing, but inwardly they are ravenous wolves. You will know them by their fruits. Do men gather grapes from thornbushes or figs from thistles? Even so, every good tree bears good fruit, but a bad tree bears bad fruit. A good tree cannot bear bad fruit, nor can a bad tree bear good fruit. Every tree that does not bear good fruit is cut down and thrown into the fire. *Therefore by their fruits you will know them.*

Not everyone who says to Me, "Lord, Lord," shall enter the kingdom of heaven, but he who does the will of My Father in heaven. Many will say to Me in that day, "Lord, Lord, have we not prophesied in Your name, cast out demons in Your name, and done many wonders in Your name?" And then I will declare to them, "I never knew you; depart from Me, you who practice lawlessness!"

Therefore whoever hears these sayings of Mine, and does them, I will liken him to a wise man who built his house on the rock: and the rain descended, the floods came, and the winds blew and beat on that house; and it did not fall, for it was founded on the rock.

But everyone who hears these sayings of Mine, and does not do them, will be like a foolish man who built his house on the sand: and the rain descended, the floods came, and the winds blew and beat on that house; and it fell. And great was its fall.

1

Test Yourself

It is a tremendous privilege for me to address you in this way.[1] In doing so, I will preach as a dying man to dying men and women and youth. I will preach as though I will never preach again, and I will tell you things that you may misunderstand. I will tell you

---

1. The material in this booklet was originally preached as a single sermon on a specific occasion. This volume is not simply a transcript of that sermon. Most of the changes involve an attempt to turn spoken, more sermonic language into written, more literary language. The aim has been to maintain the sermonic force while recognizing the constraints and embracing the capacities of the written form. All revisions have been carried out with the desire to honor the meaning of the preacher, the spiritual intent in the sermon, and, above all, the God whose Word is being proclaimed.

things that may make you angry with me, and I will tell you things that you may deny. I will tell you things that you may say I have no right to tell you. But before you come to any conclusion about what is being said here, you must ask yourself one question.

You must ask this question because preaching is a very dangerous thing. It is dangerous for me because the Bible says that false teachers will undergo greater condemnation. If what I tell you is not true, then I am in a great deal of trouble and have every right to do this with fear and trembling, because I will stand condemned before God. But if what I tell you today is true, then you have good cause for fear and trembling. If I correctly interpret this passage of Scripture that I am going to give you, it will be as though God were speaking through a man. Your problem will not be with me; it will be with God and His Word. So, here is the key question that has to be decided: Is this man before us a false prophet, or is he telling us the truth? If he is telling us the truth, then nothing else matters except conforming our lives to that truth.

We will be considering Christ's words from the seventh chapter of the Gospel of Matthew. In looking at this, I am not troubled in my heart about your self-esteem. I am not troubled in my heart about whether you feel good about yourself, whether life is turning out the way you want it to turn out, or whether your checkbook is balanced. There is only one thing for me that provokes sleepless nights. There is only one thing that troubles my soul, and it is this: within a hundred years, a great majority of people reading this little book will possibly be in hell. And many who even profess Jesus Christ as Lord will spend eternity in hell.

You ask, "How can you say such a thing?" I can say such a thing because I have done much of my Christian work outside of America. I have spent much time preaching in South America, in Africa, and in Eastern Europe. I want you to know that when you take a look at American Christianity, it is based more on a godless culture than it is on the Word of God. So many young people and adults are deceived into believing that because they prayed a prayer one time in their life, they are going to heaven. Then, when they look around at others who profess to know Christ and see those people living just as the world does, and when they compare themselves by themselves, nothing troubles their heart. They think, "Well, I am the same as most of the others in my youth group. I watch things I should not watch on television and laugh about the very things that God hates. I wear clothing that is sensual. I talk like the world. I walk like the world. I love the music of the world. I love so much that is in the world, but bless God, I am a Christian. Why am I a Christian? Well, I don't look any different from most of the other people in my church. Why am I a Christian? Because there was a time in my life when I prayed and asked Jesus Christ to come into my heart."

I want you to know that the greatest heresy in the American evangelical and Protestant church is the false idea that if you pray and ask Jesus Christ to come into your heart, He will definitely come in. You will not find that in any place in Scripture. You will not find it frequently in church history until the last century or two. What you need to know is that salvation is by faith alone in Jesus Christ. And faith alone in Jesus Christ is inseparable from repentance. Repentance is a turning away from sin; a hatred for the things that God hates and a love for the things that God loves; and a growing in holiness and in the desire not to be like the latest popular idol, like the world, like the great majority of American Christians. It is a desire to be like Jesus Christ!

You may not realize that I am addressing you. I do not say this for your approval, or to be applauded. I am speaking to you and about you.

So often people might come up to a preacher like me and say, "Oh, I'd love to

follow you into Romania" or "I'd love to follow into the Ukraine" or again "I'd love
to preach where you preached and planted
churches in Peru in the jungle."

And I tell them, "No, you wouldn't."

They say, "Yes, I would."

I say, "No, you wouldn't."

"Why?"

"Because you would be excommunicated
from the church down there."

I am not trying to be hard for the sake of
being hard. Do you realize how much love it
takes to address so many people and tell them
that American Christianity is almost totally
wrong? Do you know what it costs a man to be
cast out? To be unpopular? Do you know why
faithful preachers do it? Not because we get
paid well. Not because we are loved by people.
We do it because we love people and because,
more than that, we want to honor God.

I want to tell you something. We are
going to look into Scripture, and I want you
to consider it as it really is. This is not about

comparing yourself with others who call themselves Christians. Compare yourself to the Scriptures. When a young person comes to a pastor or a youth minister and says, "I'm not sure whether I'm saved," the youth minister will usually throw out a cliché: "Well, was there ever a time in your life when you prayed and asked Jesus to come into your heart?"

"Well, yes."

"Were you sincere?"

"Well, I don't know, but I think so."

"Well, you need to tell Satan to stop bothering you. Did you write it in the back of your Bible as the evangelist told you to do when you got saved? Did you write down the date so that any time you doubted you could point him to the Bible?"

What superstition has overcome our denominations and our churches! Do you know what the Bible tells Christians to do? Examine yourself. Test yourself in light of Scripture to see if you are in the faith. Test yourself to see if you're a Christian.

Do you realize that in many places in America and elsewhere, if you went out to knock on every door in your village, town, or city, you would find that the vast majority of people consider themselves believers? I went back to my hometown after I got saved; I knocked on every door, and do you know what I found out? Everyone in my town is a Christian. Most of them do not go to church, and those who do go to church are not concerned about holiness. They are not concerned about serving. They are not concerned about being separate from the world. They are not concerned about preaching the gospel among the nations. But yet they are confident that they are saved.

Why are they saved? Because some evangelist who should have spent less time preaching and more time studying his Bible told them they were saved, and he did it so that in his next revival he could brag about how many came forward.

2

Go through the Narrow Gate

I hope that, speaking in love, I have been able to shock you into some awareness. Now I want to go to Scripture. Listen to the Word of God and begin to ask yourself some questions. First of all, Matthew 7:13 says, "Enter by the narrow gate; for wide is the gate and broad is the way that leads to destruction, and there are many who go in by it."

There is one narrow gate. There is one God. There is one mediator between God and man—Jesus Christ. This is not a matter of multiple choice. In the ancient world they said that every road leads to Rome. But not every road leads to God. Jesus told people, "I am the way, the truth, and the life. No one comes to the Father except through Me" (John 14:6).

I praise God that the only way any human being on this earth will ever be saved is through Jesus Christ. You need to realize that the Bible warns that "all have sinned and fall short of the glory of God" (Rom. 3:23). This means that we were born radically depraved and God-hating, that we would never have sought God by ourselves. We have rebelled against God, broken every law. It is not just the fact that you have sinned. The issue is that you have never done anything but sin! The Bible says in the Prophets that even our greatest works are like filthy rags before God. And do you know what we deserve because of that? The wrath of God. The holy hatred of God.

You say, "Now, wait a minute. God doesn't hate anybody. God is love." No, my friend. You need to understand something. Jesus Christ, the prophets, and the apostles taught this: apart from the grace of God revealed in Jesus Christ our Lord, the only thing left for you is the wrath and fierce anger of God because of your rebellion and your sin.

When I preach such things in universities, students and teachers are always quick to point out, "No, God cannot hate, because God is love." And I tell you that God *must* hate because God is love. For example, I love children; therefore, I hate abortion. If I love that which is holy, I must hate that which is unholy. God is a holy God. That is something that most Americans and vast numbers of others have forgotten. Many of the things that you love to do, God hates. Did you know that?

You pray for revival. Perhaps you are going to have some great meeting. You want God to move, but before you go there you watch programs on television that God absolutely despises. And then you wonder why the Holy Spirit has not fallen on a place and why you have to create false fire and false excitement. The answer is because God is not in it! God is a holy God, and the only way you and I could ever be reconciled to a holy God is through the death of God's own Son on the cross.

If you are saved from your sins, you are not saved because the Romans and Jews rejected Jesus. You are not saved because they put a crown of thorns on His head. You are not saved because they ran a spear through His side. You are not saved because they nailed Him to a cross. Do you know why you are saved, if indeed you are saved? You are saved because when Jesus Christ was hanging on that cross, He bore your sin. The sin of God's people and all the fierce wrath of God that should have fallen on you fell on His only begotten Son. Someone had to pay that price. Someone had to die. It was God the Father who crushed His only begotten Son. According to Isaiah 53:10, "It pleased the LORD to bruise Him."

People say that the cross is a sign of how much man is worth. That is simply not true.

The cross is a sign of how depraved we really are. The only thing that could save people like us was the Son of God bearing the wrath of His own Father, paying the price for sin with His death, then rising again from the dead. These are powerful words; this is the gospel of Jesus.

What are you called to do? You must go through the narrow gate. How do you do that? Jesus said, "The time is fulfilled, and the kingdom of God is at hand." What must you do? In Mark's gospel, Christ tells us plainly: repent and believe the gospel (Mark 1:15).

Perhaps you say, "I got saved by praying and asking Jesus Christ into my heart." And I am sure you did, but you were not saved by a magic formula or some words you repeated after someone else. You were saved because you repented of your sins and believed; and not only did you do that in the past, you continue to do it even now. Jesus's call for sinners to repent and believe the good news of His kingdom might be properly paraphrased in this way: "The kingdom of God is come. The time is fulfilled. Now, spend the rest of your lives repenting of your sins and believing in Me."

Conversion is not like a flu shot. "Oh, I did that. I repented. I believed." The question is, Are you continuing to repent of sin? Are you continuing to believe? By God's grace, that is because He who began a good work in you *will* finish it.

3

Walk in the Narrow Way

We preach that you are supposed to go through that one and only gate, which is Jesus Christ. But many evangelicals have forgotten something. I want pastors and parents and youth ministers and everyone with that kind of authority and influence to consider this: we have forgotten a very important teaching in God's gospel. Not only is the gate narrow; so is the path. What we basically do is lead people to Christ, lead them in a prayer, and then they spend the rest of their lives living just like the fallen world. If you doubt me on this, I can bring statistics to prove you wrong. When Gallup polls, Barna polls, or any other polls you can possibly look at compare the

morality of the American church with the
morality of those who do not claim Christ,
they find little difference in lifestyle. That has
nothing to do with religious interpretation.
Those are merely the bald statistics.

Book after book is being churned out by
theologian and philosopher and sociologist
alike. What has happened to the church? We
find out that abortion in the church is nearly
as prevalent as in the world. We find that
unbiblical divorce is nearly as prevalent. We
find that immorality is rampant. You know
as well as I do that there are many—perhaps
even you who are reading this sermon—
who practice immorality and yet worship
God in the church. There are young people
who are abusing drugs yet strolling along
to their youth groups. Professing Christians
are watching and doing things that are not
appropriate for a Christian, yet they are coming to the youth group, believing themselves
satisfied, believing themselves saved, and
few are saying anything except this: "They're

carnal Christians. They're really Christians; they're just carnal." That was a doctrine that started in an American Baptist seminary several decades ago. It is not biblical and it is not historical. My dear friend, there is no such thing as a carnal Christian.

Some might respond, "Now wait a minute! What about 1 Corinthians, chapter 3? 'Are ye not carnal?' The apostle Paul said that."

Yes, that is what Paul said. But you need to read the whole book to find out what he meant! You see, one of our massive problems is that most of our Christianity is based on clichés that we read on the back of Christian T-shirts. So much of our Christianity comes from songwriters and not the Bible. Most of what we believe is dictated to us through our culture and not by the Bible. The Bible never teaches that a person can be a genuine Christian and live in continuous carnality and wickedness, sinning all the days of his or her life. The Bible actually teaches that the genuine Christian has been given a new nature.

Genuine Christians have a heavenly Father who loves them, disciplines them, watches over them, and cares for them.

My heart is breaking because you know this as well as I do. Let us not be hypocrites about it! Let us not hide it! There are so many who are falling into this trap. You know them. You might be one of them, or you at least know that they are in your church or youth group. They do all this religious stuff, but in their heart they are nearly as wicked as wicked can be. There is no difference between them and anyone else in the world. There is no light. Everything that the world does, they do, and they think it is appropriate. As far as they are concerned, it is all okay. My friend, that is *not* Christianity. They are not merely in danger of losing their reward. They are in danger of hell. They do not know God.

What is missing from our teaching? When was the last time you heard someone say that there is not only a narrow gate into heaven but also and only a narrow way? Jesus indicates

that one of the principal signs of being a genuine Christian is that you walk in the narrow
way. Do you know what the sign for being a
genuine Christian is in much of America? You
prayed a prayer one time. Is that not amazing?
What are you then asked if you doubt your
salvation? "Did you pray a prayer one time?"
But listen to what Scripture teaches! "Examine
yourselves as to whether you are in the faith"
(2 Cor. 13:5). Test yourselves in the light of
Scripture to see if you're in the path, because a
Christian will be different.

Am I saying that a Christian is without sin? No, because in 1 John we learn that
Christians do sin, and that if any man does
not acknowledge his sin, he does not know
God. That man is not walking in the light. So
what is the difference? What am I really getting at? Simply this: that if you are genuinely
a born-again Christian, a child of God, you
will walk in the way of righteousness as a lifestyle—a way of life. And if you step off that
path of righteousness, the Father will come

for you. He will discipline you. He will put you back on that path. However, if you profess to have gone through the narrow gate but you actually live in the broad way—living like all the other people in your high school, or workplace, just like all the other people who are carnal and wicked—then the Bible wants you to know that you should be terribly, terribly afraid because you do not know God.

I fear for those who have spent most of their lives telling other people that they are saved. I fear for you if you have done that. The preacher's task is not to tell people that they are saved; the preacher tells people how to be saved. God tells them that they are saved. What we have forgotten is that salvation is a supernatural work of God. Those who have genuinely been converted, regenerated by the power of the Holy Spirit, are going to be new creatures. The Bible says, "If anyone is in Christ, he is a new creation" (2 Cor. 5:17). So it is that we find in Scripture that there is a narrow gate and a narrow way to everlasting life.

4

You Will Know Them by Their Fruit

Now look at Matthew 7:15–16: "Beware of false prophets, who come to you in sheep's clothing, but inwardly they are ravenous wolves. You will know them by their fruits." A long time ago, a wise man told me, "Your best friend is the one who tells you the most truth about yourself." You need to realize this. In America, we have become so thin-skinned that no one can rebuke us. No one can tell us that we are wrong. Ministers and leaders alike have bought into this lie. We do not want to offend. We want to be seeker friendly. What you need to realize is there is only one true seeker, and He is God. If you want to be friendly to someone in your church, you need to be friendly to God. You need to be more concerned for the glory of God than you are for the attitudes of men. You also need to grasp that the person who loves you the most will tell you the most truth about yourself and about God.

One of the greatest distinguishing marks of a false prophet is that he will always tell you what you want to hear. He will never rain on your parade. He will get you clapping. He will get you jumping. He will make you dizzy. He will keep you entertained, and he will present a Christianity to you that will make your church look like a Jesus-based amusement park. He will keep you so entertained that you are never addressed with great issues such as these: Is God working in my life? Am I growing in holiness? Have I truly been born again?

If all the people in a community or even a church believe themselves saved, and we know that this is not true from Scripture, because the Bible says that few will enter in, how do *you* truly know that *you* are saved? Is it because someone told you? Because you prayed a prayer? Because you believed? Let me ask you a question. How do you know that you believed? After all, the majority of people say that they believe, regardless of the lack of fruit in their lives. How do you know that you are not like them? Do you know what the Bible teaches about how you can know if you are saved? Do you know how, up until about fifty years ago, faithful ministers would have told you how you know you have been saved? You have assurance of your salvation because you both trust in God's promises and your life is in the process of being changed, and your style of life is one of walking in the paths of God's truth.

When a real Christian steps off those paths of righteousness and begins to walk in disobedience, as we all prove to do, God comes for you and puts you back on the path. One of the greatest evidences that you have truly been born again is that God will not let you walk as your flesh might want to talk. God will not let you dress as the sensual world and the sensual church allow you to dress. God will not allow you to act like the world, smell like the world, speak like the world, listen to the things that the world listens to. God will make a difference in your life.

Christ says, "You will know them by their fruits" (Matt. 7:16). How will you know a false prophet? In the wider application, confirmed by the rest of Scripture, how will you know if someone is a genuine Christian? By their fruit, my dear friend. Look at your life. Look at the way you walk. Look at the way you talk. Look at the passions of your heart. Is Jesus in there somewhere? Or is He just some accessory that you add on to your life? Is He just something that you do on Wednesday or Sunday? Is He someone or something that you give only a mental assent to? Or is He the very center of your life? And what is the fruit that you are bearing? Do you look like the world? Do you act like the world?

Do you have and experience the same joys as the world experiences? Can you love sin and relish it? Can you love rebellion and relish it? Then you do not know God! You will know them by their fruit. God has the power to change a sinner's heart, and that always changes the life.

Imagine, for a moment, being present when Jesus taught this passage. You are sitting out there listening. The Lord looks at you. He says, "Thistles, thistles. Do you find thistles on fig trees?"

And you respond, "Of course not, Jesus. Everybody knows that you do not find thistles on fig trees."

"Well, then, let me ask you another question. Do you find figs—good fruit—on thorn trees?"

"Why, no, Jesus. That is absolutely ludicrous. I mean, you are never going to find thorns on a fig tree, and you are not going to find figs on a thorn tree. To think that it could be possible—well, anyone who tells you that, Jesus, you can mark it down…that man is either crazy or he is a liar."

And then Jesus comes back to you: "Well then, those who call themselves my disciples and bear bad fruit, would not it be the same to say that they were either lying or out of their mind to make such a statement?"

Let me take this a little further. Imagine that I show up late for a preaching engagement and I run up onto the platform, and all the leaders are angry with me and say, "Don't you appreciate the fact that you are given an opportunity to speak here? And yet you come late!"

I might reply, "Brothers, you have to forgive me."

"Why?" they ask.

"Well, I was out here driving on the highway, and I had a flat tire. When I was changing the tire, the lug nut fell off. I wasn't paying attention that I was on the highway, and I ran out and grabbed the lug nut. I picked it up in the middle of the highway, but when I stood up there was a thirty-ton logging truck going one hundred miles an hour about ten yards in front of me. That truck ran me over, and that's why I'm late."

I know few people study logic anymore, but there would be only two logical conclusions you could draw. First, I am a liar or, second, I am a madman. You would probably say to me, "That is absolutely absurd. It is impossible to have an encounter with something as large as a logging truck and not be changed."

And so my question to you would be, "Which is larger? A logging truck or God?" How is it, then, that so many people today profess to have had an encounter with Jesus Christ, but they are not permanently changed? Let me give you a few things to think about. You know that I am telling you the truth. How many times do some go and "rededicate their lives" over and over and over again? How many times do youth groups go to conferences, but when people

go back to their church after getting fired
up, their enthusiasm lasts about a week and
a half? And yet we claim, "Oh, it was a great
movement of God." No, it was not! If it does
not last, it was not a great movement of God.
It was emotional. It was so many things, but it
was not a great movement of God. Has God
worked in your life? Is God working in your
life? "You will know them by their fruit."

Christ goes on to say that every tree that
does not bear good fruit is cut down and
thrown into the fire; therefore, you will know
them by their fruit (Matt. 7:19–20). You need
to understand something about Hebrew
literature to fully grasp this. When you and
I want to emphasize something, what do we
do? If we are speaking, we raise our voice.
If we are writing, we put it in bold letters or
italicize it. But to a Jew, it is different. When
he wants to emphasize something, he repeats
it and repeats it.

That is why you find what we call Hebrew
parallelisms in the book of Proverbs and

elsewhere. For example, we might be told something like "the wicked will be cut off from the earth, and the unfaithful will be uprooted from it" (Prov. 2:22). The writer is saying the same thing, just doing so in a slightly different way to give greater emphasis. That is what the Lord Jesus is doing over and over again here: you will know them by their fruit. You will know them by the path that they walk in. He further says, "Every tree that does not bear good fruit is cut down and thrown into the fire" (Matt. 7:19). What is He talking about? He is talking about the judgment of almighty God that will one day fall on the world, that will one day fall possibly on you.

Dear friend, I cannot look into your heart. I am so easily deceived by my own heart, but there is One who is not deceived. There is One who is not deceived by contemporary Christian culture. He knows. You will know them by their fruit.

5

Fruitless Professions of Faith

The Lord Jesus warns us, "Not everyone who says to Me, 'Lord, Lord,' shall enter the kingdom of heaven, but he who does the will of My Father in heaven" (Matt. 7:21). Do you know what your profession of faith in Jesus Christ is worth if you don't bear fruit by doing the will of the Father? Absolutely nothing. Did you read that passage? Study it. Not everyone who comes to Christ and says, "Lord, Lord," will enter into the kingdom of heaven. Not all who make a public profession of following Christ are Christians on their way to glory. There are many people who are going to profess, "Lord, Lord," but they are not going to enter into the kingdom of heaven. Could it be that you are one of them?

Let us again go back to Hebrew literature. Christ spoke of those who say "Lord, Lord." He didn't say "Lord" just once. What does that mean? The fellow who is making this profession is not someone who all of a sudden decided, "The judgment is coming and I had better profess Jesus to be Lord." This is a person who emphatically declares to other people that Jesus Christ is Lord. He walks around saying "Lord." He sings movingly up in front while the musicians are playing, saying "Lord." He sings the songs and says "Lord." But Jesus will say to him, "I never knew you; depart from Me" (Matt. 7:23).

Billy Graham was one of the kindest, most loving men. Even so, he said he believed that a great majority of people who attend Bible-believing churches are lost. He said that he would be happy if even 5 percent of all the people who made professions of faith in his campaigns are even saved.

I have visited a mother in Nigeria whose son was in our church and martyred by the Muslims. In northern Nigeria, when someone professes faith in Jesus Christ, you know that person might soon die because of that profession. That gives their testimony some credibility! But what of America? How we need to consider the cost. Think! Examine your life in light of Scripture. Do you know the Lord? Not everyone who says to him "Lord, Lord" will enter the kingdom of heaven. What does it say in the Bible? "Not everyone who says to Me, 'Lord, Lord,' shall enter the kingdom of heaven, but he who does the will of My Father in heaven."

What is the sign that someone has become a genuine Christian? I wish that we would start teaching this again. What happened to our theology? What happened to our doctrine? What happened to our teaching? It went right out the window. No one wants to study doctrine anymore. People just want to listen to songs and read the back of

Christian T-shirts. What happened to truth? Truth tells you this: the evidence—the way that you can have assurance that you are genuinely a born-again Christian—is that your lifestyle conforms to the will of the Father.

You might say, "Oh, you're just talking about works." No, I am not! I'm talking about evidence of faith, and it goes like this: your profession of faith is no proof that you are born again, because so many in America profess faith in Jesus Christ. The pollster Barna tells us that 65 to 70 percent of all Americans think they are saved, born-again Christians. And yet we look like one of the most godless countries on the face of the earth! We kill four thousand babies a day, but, supposedly, 70 percent of us are born again. How do you know that the faith you have is not false? Where is the style of life that is concerned about doing the will of the Father, that practices the will of the Father? When a Christian disobeys the will of the Father, the Holy Spirit comes and reprimands that believer either personally through the written Word of God or through a brother or sister in Christ, and God puts His child back on the path again. If you are a genuine Christian, you cannot escape Him.

Let me give you an example. Suppose I were your pastor and you were fourteen years old, and I came back from preaching at one o'clock in the morning and saw you standing out there in a park or on a street corner with a bunch of hoodlums, doing things you should not be doing. If you are a member of our church, I would tell you, "Get in the car." I would take you home to your father. I would not be mad at you. I would be mad at your father! I would tell him, "Sir, you are a derelict father for allowing your child to be out in such circumstances."

I want you to know something. God is not a derelict father. If you can play around in sin, if you can love the world and the things of the world, if you can always be involved in the world and doing the things of the world, if your heroes are worldly people, if you want to look like them and act like them, if you practice the same things they practice, then please heed my words: there is a good chance that you do not truly know God and that you do not belong to Him.

6

Does Jesus Know You?

See what else the Lord Jesus says: "Many will say to Me in that day, 'Lord, Lord, have we not prophesied in Your name, cast out demons in Your name, and done many wonders in Your name?' And then I will declare to them, 'I never knew you; depart from Me, you who practice lawlessness!'" (Matt. 7:22–23).

You say that the most important thing on the face of the earth is to know Jesus Christ. That is not true. The most important thing is that Jesus Christ knows you. I am not going to get into the White House tomorrow because I walk up to the gate and tell everybody that I know the president. They would let me in if the president comes out and points at me and says, "I know that man."

You can profess to know Jesus, but my question for you is not only "Do you know Jesus?" but also "Does Jesus know you?" Look how the Lord Christ describes the lost man here. He said, "Depart from Me, you who practice lawlessness!" In Greek, the word is *anomia*. It is made up of two elements: the negative particle, *a*, a negation, with the root word *nomos*, which means "law." It describes someone who is "without law." This is what the whole phrase means when translated accurately, and I wish that I could be with you to put my arms around you as I communicate this: Jesus will say to those who practice lawlessness, "Depart from me, those of you who claim to be my disciples, those who confessed me as Lord, but who live as though I never gave you a law to obey."

I have just described the great majority of North American Christians. I am describing the vast majority of modern evangelicals around the world. If anyone starts talking about law, if anyone starts talking about biblical principles identifying what we are supposed to do and not to do, how we are to live and how we ought not to live, everyone starts screaming, "Legalist!" But Jesus said, "Depart from me those of you who live lawlessly—you called me Lord, but you lived as though I had never given a law."

In so much modern Christianity in the West today, we just pass through the gate and shout, "Praise God!" Then we live like the rest of the world and act as if all is well. "You're just carnal," we suggest. "Maybe one day you'll come back." Do you know what happens because of our bad evangelism? We have countless thousands of children who we claim are saved in vacation Bible school. When the great majority of them become fifteen years old, they enter into the world and live like demons! Then when they are around thirty years old, they come back and rededicate their lives. It may be that they only just got saved, but they still need a life that demonstrates that fact. Christianity is more than just telling people they are saved because they acknowledge that Jesus is Lord. Satan acknowledges that Jesus is Lord! Is your life in a process of change?

7

Two Kinds of People

Christ then concludes by talking about two people. He speaks of two foundations. We need to understand this correctly, which is why it is important to study theology and history. The contemporary interpretation of this passage about the rock and the sand is basically this: "If you are a Christian, you need to build your life on the rock because if you build your life on the sand, you'll be an unhappy Christian and your life will not go right." That is *not* what Jesus is teaching, and the history of interpretation backs me up. It was hardly ever interpreted that way.

Let me give you the true interpretation. There are two ways. There is a narrow way and a broad way. Which way are you on? There are two types of trees. There is a good tree that bears good fruit—a man going to heaven. There is a bad tree that you know is bad because it bears bad fruit—a man going to hell. That tree is going to be cut down and thrown into the fire. There are those who profess Jesus as Lord and do the will of the Father who is in heaven. There are those who profess that Jesus Christ is Lord but who do not do the will of the Father who is in heaven. And they go to hell—not because of a lack of works but because of a lack of faith that is demonstrated by their lack of works.

The Lord Jesus goes on. He makes clear that this is not a picture of two Christians building their houses on two different foundations. No! This is a saved man and a lost man. The lost man hears the Word of God preached, but he lays no foundation. You cannot see in any way how the Word of God is forming and building and sustaining his life. His life bears no relation to God's truth. How

many people in our big denominations—
regardless of all our numbers, regardless of
everything we say, if we were to simply compare our people to this passage—would have
any real hope of salvation? What if I asked,
"Are you building your marriage on the Word
of God? Are you raising your children on
the Word of God? Are you regulating your
finances on the Word of God? Are you living
separately from the things of this world based
on the Word of God?" How many would be
able to answer positively?

But there is none of that! Instead, we
hear, "I profess Jesus. He's my Savior. My
Sunday school teacher told me so." Leonard
Ravenhill, an acquaintance of mine before he
passed on, used to say, "I preach in a lot of
Baptist churches once." I too preach in a lot
of places once. I could get up on the platform,
or stand behind the pulpit, with a vocabulary
that would astound you, and I could preach
things that would lift you up and float you
around the room. I could tell you stories that

would make you laugh and stories about dogs and grandmas that would make you cry, but I love my hearers too much to preach that, and I love you too much to write it. I know, because the Word of God is true, that there are people who believe themselves to be saved who are not truly saved.

I know that there are some of you who look at others and think, "Well, I'm saved. I mean, I look like everybody else in my youth group." What makes you think those others are saved? "Well, I'm like my parents." Or perhaps you'll say, "I'm like the adults in my church or the deacon or the pastor." What does that matter? You won't be judged by them on the day of Christ's coming. My question for you has to do with your soul and your relationship to God in Christ. I pray that some day when my children grow up, a preacher will stand before them and expose the emptiness of so much worldly religion, and say, "Enough of this nonsense! Let us get down to business! What does the

Word of God say? How does your life stand in the light of that final day, in front of that blazing fire which is the holiness of God?"

Beloved friend, on that final day, will your confession hold true? Are you saved? I am not talking about some vague idea: "Well, I think I'm saved." Do you know that there is a way that seems right to a man, but it leads unto death?

"Well," someone might say, "I feel in my heart of hearts that I'm saved." Then let me ask you a question. Did you ever read that the heart is deceitfully wicked—who can know it? Should you not turn to the testimony of Scripture rather than the instinct of your fallen heart?

Another says, "I know I'm saved because my mom, my dad, my pastor, everybody else told me I was saved." So I am asking you this: What does the Word of God tell you?

8

Real Holiness

We talk so much about being radical Christians. Radical Christians are not people who jump around at concerts. Radical Christians are not people who just wear Christian T-shirts. Radical Christians are those who bear the fruit of the Holy Spirit. Radical Christians are those who reverence and honor their parents even when they feel that their parents are wrong. Radical Christians are those who do not dress sensually in order to show off their bodies. If your clothing is a frame for your face, God is pleased with your clothing. If your clothing is a frame for your body, it is merely sensual, and God hates what you are doing.

I am talking about Christianity! I have spent my life in jungles. I have spent my life freezing in the Andes Mountains. I have seen people die. I have seen a little boy shot by Muslims five times through the stomach and left on a sidewalk, simply because he cried out, "I am so afraid, but I cannot deny Jesus Christ. Please don't kill me, but I will not deny Him." That boy died in a pool of blood. And you talk about being a radical Christian because you go to a conference! I am talking about real holiness. I am talking about true godliness.

What would a movement of God among us involve? It would mean that we all came under conviction of sin; that we all fell down on our faces and wept because we watch the things that God hates, wear the things that God hates, act like the world, look like the world, smell like the world; that we began to mourn over doing the very things that grieve God and being unaware of our sinfulness and our shallow knowledge of His Word.

Even though we claim that the Scriptures are the infallible Word of God, all we get in preaching is unbiblical illustrations, stories, and quaint little tales. Oh, that God would shine on us, that we would turn away from our sin, that we would renounce the things that are displeasing to Him, that we would run to Him, relish Him, and love Him!

I pray that God would raise up missionaries today. I do not wish the same things that others might want for you. Your parents might want for you to have security and insurance and nice homes. They want you to have cars and respect. I want for you the same thing that I want for my son—that one day he takes the spiritual banner of Jesus Christ and preaches the Word of God, placing the gospel banner on a hill where no one has ever placed that banner before. I want him to cry out, "Jesus Christ is Lord," even if it costs my son his life. What if he says to me the same thing I said when I was a young man: "I'm going into the mountains.

I'm going into the jungle." People said to me, "You can't go there. You're insane. It's a war. You're going to die." Should my son grow up and put on that backpack to go, I am going to pray over him and say, "Go! God be with you, and if you die, my son, I will see you in glory and I will honor your death."

9

What Is Your Response?

In light of these things, do you need to confess, "I have been living a lie. I claim to be a Christian but I love the world, and I look like it and smell like it and I hate myself for it. I am so tired of this so-called Christianity that I am living. I am sick of it, and I want to be saved"? If that is so, repent of your sins now; come to Jesus Christ for the forgiveness of your sins and the granting of everlasting life.

What of those who claim to be Christians? Does your life honor Jesus Christ? Are you looking in His Word to find out how you are supposed to live? There are really only two possibilities for the purifying of the professing church in the modern West.

The first possibility is a total reformation in our preaching and our study of the Word of God; the other is fierce, horrifying persecution. Only these things will purify Christ's church. I pray that you would return to the Word. You need to know. You need to say, "Okay, how am I supposed to live before my parents?" Go into the Word, find out, obey it. "How am I supposed to dress?" Go into the Word, find out, obey it. "How am I supposed to talk? What am I supposed to listen to?" Bring every thought, word, and deed into subjection to Jesus Christ.

If you are reading this book and are embracing its truth, I want you to live for Jesus Christ with all your heart, right where you are. Perhaps you say, "I want to live for Jesus Christ, but I don't know how." Tell your pastor and ask for help. If you do not have a faithful pastor, find one and tell him. If you do not have a pastor at all, find a faithful one and tell him! It will soon be clear if your desire to follow Christ is real. How? Because it will last. That is the way we know that it is from God.

If Christ has genuinely called you to Himself and given you a new heart, that will last. If you listen to a sermon or read a book and make a few surface changes but after a few weeks you go right back into the world and live like the world, it is because nothing really changed. You may have got emotion, but that is about it. If you really received something from the Lord, it will endure. Even if you were to try to run away from it, you would not be able to do so.

Do you say, "I need to know Jesus Christ"? Then call on Him, enter through the narrow gate, and you shall be saved. Do you say, "I need to follow Jesus Christ"? Then cling to Him, walk along the narrow way, and you shall reach glory at last.

A Closing Prayer

Oh, God, I do not care about reputation. I do not care what men think. I want You to be honored. I want sinners to be saved. I want those who are saved to stop looking around at a cultural Christianity that You hate and will spew out of Your mouth. I want them to look at the Word of God and say, "I will follow Jesus."

I pray for pastors, that You would fill them with the spirit of wisdom and love and boldness and discernment. And dear God, whatever the cost, I pray that You will raise up missionaries. Save our children and raise them up and send them even into the worst part of the battle. Raise up preachers and pastors and evangelists who know the Word of God. Oh God, please work among us! Amen.